1000+ Must Know Words in Ebira/Igbira

Illustrated Ebira/Igbira-English Dictionary

by Adamu Atta

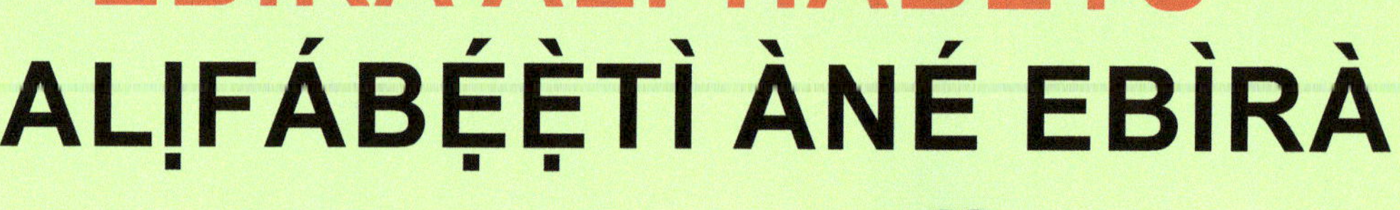

EBIRA ALPHABETS – ALỊFÁBẸẸTÌ ÀNÉ EBÌRÀ

A Àdá
Father

Ạ Ạga
Chair

B Bányí
Giant

C Chàkúu
Darkness

E Epehù
Okra

Ẹ Ẹza
Bean

G Gara
To scatter

D Dẹẹre
Slender

H Hyéyi
Surprised

I Izinkaha
Rice

Ị Ịra
Fire

J Jee
To wait

K Kiiki
To be small

M Mi
To quench

N Nẹba
To be high

Ng Ngụ
To enter

Ny Nyinyi
To laugh

O OKutẹ
Walking Stick

Ọ Ọpa
Arrow

P Pataki
Very much

R Ràrà
Bend

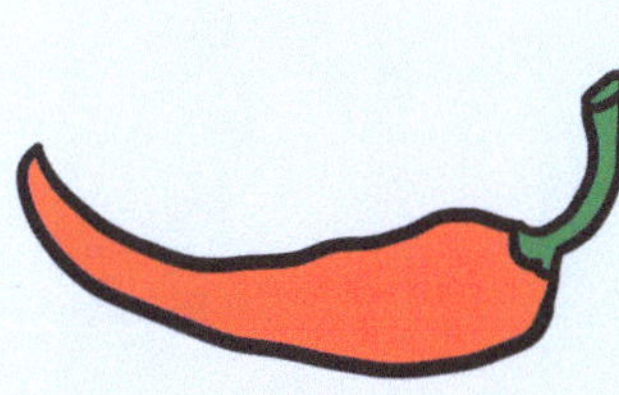

S Shumbo
Cayenne Pepper

U Uji
Basket

Ụ Ukokoro
Key

V Vara
To change

T Tatashe
Bell Pepper

W Wèyí
Small

Y Yaaịtẹ
Sit down

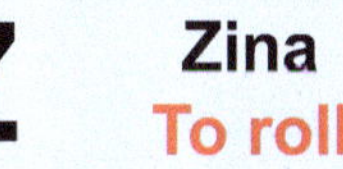

Z Zina
To roll

NUMBERS – ÌRÌKÀ

½	Àchéva One-half
⅓	Àchétá One-third
¼	Àchénà One-fourth
0	Òsùsù Zero
1	Ọ̀ọnyị One
2	Ẹ̀ẹva Two
3	Ẹ̀ẹtá Three
4	Ẹ̀ẹnà Four
5	Ẹ̀ẹhí Five
6	Hìnọnyị/ Ìhìnọnyị Six
7	Hímba/Ìhímba Seven
8	Hínta/Ìhínta Eight
9	Hịìnà/Ìhíìna Nine
10	Ẹ̀ẹwụ́ Ten
11	Ẹ̀wụrọ́nyâ Eleven
12	Ẹ̀wụrẹva Twelve
13	Ẹ̀wụrẹta Thirteen
14	Ẹ̀wụrẹnà Fourteen
15	Ẹ̀wụrẹ́hị Fifteen
16	Ẹ̀wụrịhìnọnyị Sixteen
17	Ẹ̀wụrịhímba Seventeen

18	Ẹ̀wụrịhịnta Eighteen
19	Ẹ̀wụrịhịìnà Nineteen
20	Òòhu Twenty
25	Oohu Rẹhi Twenty Five
30	Òhurẹ̀ẹwụ Thirty
35	Oohu Rẹwu Rẹhi Thirty Five
40	Ẹbẹ̀ẹva Forty
50	Ẹ̀várẹ̀wú Fifty
60	Ẹbẹẹ̀tá Sixty
70	Ẹ̀tárẹwụ Seventy
80	Ẹbẹẹnà Eighty
90	Ẹẹna rẹwu Ninety
100	Ẹchẹ́hị One Hundred
200	Ireka Two Hundred
300	Irekeechehi Three Hundred
400	Irekaakava Four Hundred
500	Irekavarechehi Five Hundred
600	Irekaakata Six Hundred

700	Irekakata-rechehi Seven Hundred
800	Irekakana Eight Hundred
900	Irekaakana-rechehi Nine Hundred
1,000	Irekaakahi One Thousand
1,100	Irekakahi-rechehi One Thousand One Hundred
1,200	Irekakahi-rechireka One Thousand Two Hundred
1,300	Irekakahi-rechirekechehi One Thousand Three Hundred
1,400	Irekakahi-rechirekeva One Thousand Four Hundred
1,500	Irekakahi-rechireke-varechehi One Thousand Five Hundred
1,600	Irekakahi-rechireketa One Thousand Six Hundred
1,700	IIrekakahi-rechi-rekechehi One Thousand Seven Hundred
1,800	Irekakahi-rechiakana One Thousand Eight Hundred
1,900	Irekakahi-rechienarehi One Thousand Nine Hundred
2,000	Irekakawu Two Thousand
3,000	Irekakawu-rakahi Three Thousand
1,000,000	Irekechenya One Million
1,000,000,000	Irekechenyeta One Billion

PARTS OF THE BODY – ẸGẸ ẸNGWỤÀNÁ ỊNÍ ẸNGWỤ́

MONTHS OF THE YEAR – ỤHỤẸ̀ÀNÁ ỊNÍ ỊRAYÍ

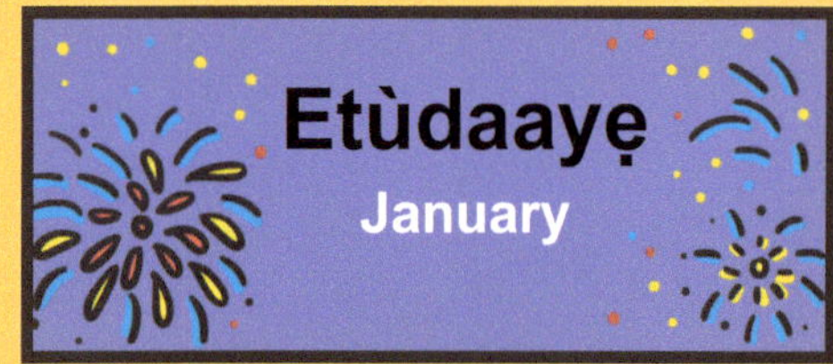

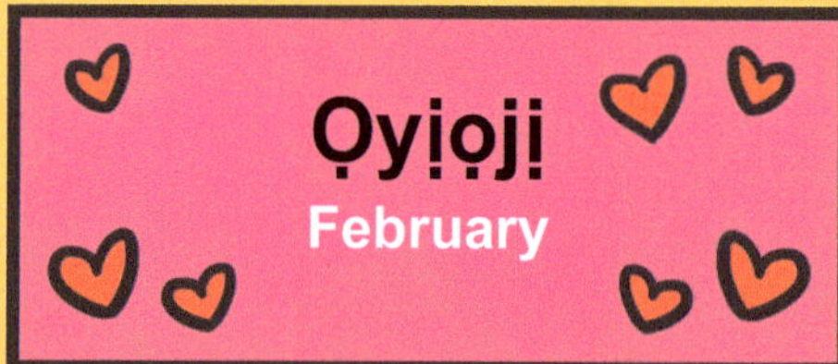

DAYS OF THE WEEK – ẸKỤHÎ ÀNÁ ỊNÍ ỌSẸ

Àmóto
Sunday

Ọsi'nyhimà
Monday

Àsụvurí
Tuesday

Iviovi/Ihiovi
Wednesday

Àsipita
Thursday

Opotu
Friday

Ụhuotu
Saturday

COLO(U)RS – ỌDÀ/ACHERE

Ojoójî/Oji
Black

Ìpuple/Ọrẹ̀
Purple

Ọdà oni atítọ́
Gray/Ash

Ọnídàádụ
Brown

Oni Ụrẹ́/Angẹrẹ/
Ọrọọrẹ/Ẹrẹẹrẹ
Green

Igóòru/I(U)suu
Gold

Ọdà oni Òròmí/Ọnakọkọ
Orange

Ìpịnkí/Ọnatiti
Pink

Igóòru Ọ́vụ̂
Silver

Ọ́vuọọvû
White

Ọdà oni ụhụẹ́/
Odozeyirị
Yellow

Ovíví
Red

Ìvùrû
Blue

EMOTIONS – EZÈMÀ

Hínayí/Ayi Ohine/Uje/
Ayohine
Happy/Happiness

Ànyì kụ/Oyiku
Angry

Ayíodú
Sad

Ayíhụ́ríné/Angwahị
Scared/Fear

Hụ́rayíné
Worried

Hyéyi
Surprised

Ụhá
Tired

Ẹngwụ́ọ́zi
Sick

SEASON – Ụ̀MỆ

Ìrẹ̀sụ̀
Rainy Season

Ụ̀mẹ̀ ẹtẹ́ ohúnẹ́nè
Winter/Cold Season

Ọ̀gụ̀
Harmattan

Ọsìnàgẹrị
Drought

Ọháhị
Dry Season

Ịnyanya
Lightning

WEATHER – ẸTỌVÀRÀ

Opómi/Okoruwa
Storm/Hurricane

Oríhî/
Ihineba
Rain

Ọ̀gáázị
Rainbow

Àpáànà Ìinebá/
Iritu
Thunder

Ọ̀hàrà
Flood

Ọyị/ Ọyị aàhá
Sun/Sunny

Inyinyi'/Ègùhi
Ice/Snow

Ahị
Breeze/Windy

MY HOUSE – IRÉHI ÁMỊ

Ịpáànụ
Roof
Òdódó - Flower
Ụhùòtò ịní ùgènè
Picture on the wall
Òzè/Ukere
Door
Ira/Arásị
Fire/
Fireplace
Òzékẹtẹ
Window
Ìjóngò
Bottle
Òré
Mirror
Ẹ̀para
Body Lotion
Ọchọtọ
Toothbrush
Ọpámẹ
Shelf
Ụ̀sì ìhìẹ̀rè
Toilet
Òsírehí-húnẹ́nẹ̀
Air conditioner
Ịrakótùpà/ Òzótùpà
Lamp
Ọbajuroko
Radio
Àpótíroye
Computer
Ọjáhí/Ịpẹpẹ
Fan
Enyi óhúnẹnẹ́
Cold Water
Àhọhuényi
Bathroom
àchì oyi
nyèé ẹngwụ́
Towel
Anyi ọgwuịrá
Hot Water
Ụ̀kụ̀ọ̀
Soap
Ìkònkọ̀/Awe'
Sponge
Irego
High Grass

ON THE FARM –
ỊNÍ AARẸ

FRUITS, NUTS & VEGETABLES – ẸTỤ́TỤ̀Ọ́CHÌ, AVÍ OYI NÈ ẸPẸ̀ỌNÌRÌ ÙHÚ

Atárà
Bitter Kola
Àrìvásà
Onion
Atárodo
Habanero peppers/
Scotch Bonnet
Ìgàlịkị
Garlic
Ẹza/Ẹbanjẹjẹ
Beans
Ịhyẹmíhyẹmẹ̀/
Oduku
Potato
Ìmángòrò oyìvó
Hog Plum
Ìgingár
Ginger
Ịrẹgụn/
Ìrèngwá
Paw-paw
Ẹ́tụ́pà
Peanuts/
Groundnuts
Ìrù/Uru
Mushroom
Ọ̀gẹ́dẹ̀
Banana
Ụjị
Sugarcane
Ịnyaakụ
Garden Egg
Arùsá
Walnut
Ụnẹ/Ùne
Locust Beans
Ịpapara
Melon Seeds
Ẹhuọ
Spinach
Shumbo
Cayenne Pepper
Akọ́kọ ojoójî
Black Peppers
Ẹ̀pòyìvó
Pineapple

ANIMALS – ỊSỤPÁ

Àràhị
Spider
Àvùtá/Adupo
Lizard
Ìsì
Housefly
Ikù
Scorpion
Ìgòngò/
Ọgọdọbẹ
Ostrich
Àgụ́gụ̀
Crocodile
Ọ̀pàrị/Aparị
Mosquito
Iride/Irivutene
Snail
Èkùeejé
Squirrel
Ahịhị
Cockroach
Ìkàzì
Ladybug
Òchòóchóno
Peacock
Ọ̀pàkụ́
Tortoise
Ìkùrúngù/Ụhịga
Shark
Ìrèrè
Electric Fish
Úsú/Isu/Ahịna
Rat/Mouse

Ọdọba
Elephant
Ẹ́dọ/Akono/
Aravode
Antelope
Idù
Lion
Ọ̀dụ̀mí
Hyena
Ịkẹ́rịkẹ́tẹ́
Donkey
Àkàtàporo
Cheetah
Ẹzụ/Ama
Tiger
Ùmáátà
Zebra
Àmà
Serval Cat
Ọkávụ́/Ịnọkị
Gorilla
Àjàbonoko
Rhinoceros
Ẹya
Buffalo
Ịnyaakụmịnavị/Ọ̀gọ́dọbẹ
Giraffe

PROFESSION – ỌKÀ ỌNI ỤKỌRỌ

Okiwe òbányí
Professor
Ọ̀zà àná gẹ́ àchì
Fashion Designer
Onuye
Butcher
Ọ̀mịchákànda Iréhi
Architect
Anịngẹ́rẹ̀
Blacksmith
Ọ̀zà àná mí írá
Fireman
Ọme àhọ̀nọ̀ òyìvó
Pharmacist
Ọ̀zùbè Ìvòvò
Fisherman
Ịtíchà
Teacher
Ọ̀zà àná shéyipeè atẹ́mẹ́
Shepherd
Oserubazị
Doctor
Ọwà Arépírénì
Pilot

Ọbẹ́ igóòru
Miner
Òzùbè/Onube
Hunter
Òni ụkọ́rọ́
enyúsẹ́
Welder
Òdọzịréyí kà
Journalist
Ọ̀zà àná sì
ìrùvò ịréyí
Scientist
Òmààhè
irenu òhinê
Actor
Ọ̀zẹ̀kẹ̀hì ìrìkà
Accountant
Ọ̀kụ́rẹ́sụ́
Barber
Òmààhè
irenu òhinê
Comedian
Ọ̀chẹ̀riwe
Author
Ọ̀mịsọ́ọ́rị
Chef

MODES OF TRANSPORTATION – ÒZÈ Ọ̀NỌ̀ Ọ̀ZÀ AÀ ZỊ JỊNẸ̀

BUILDING – IRÉHI

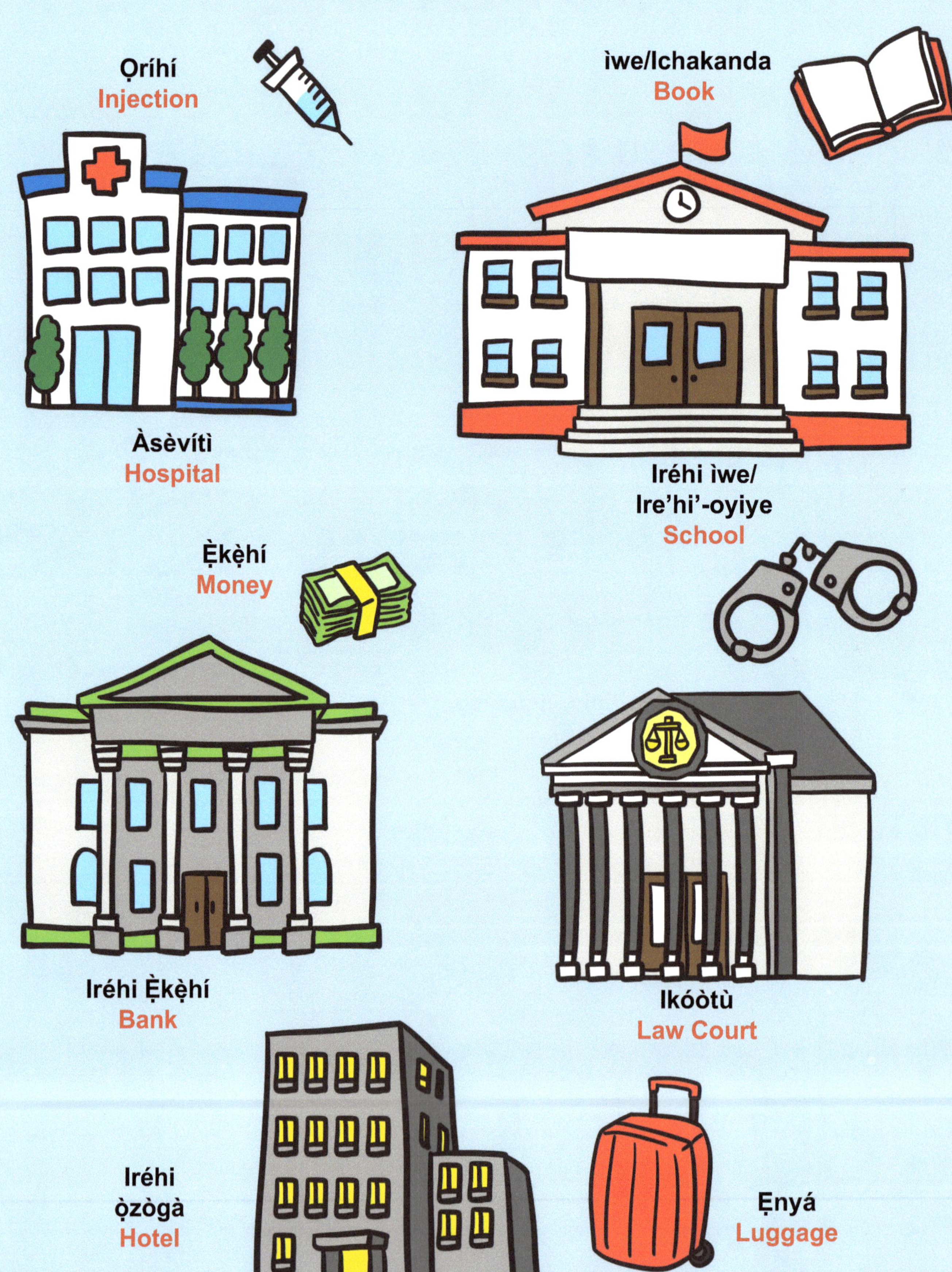

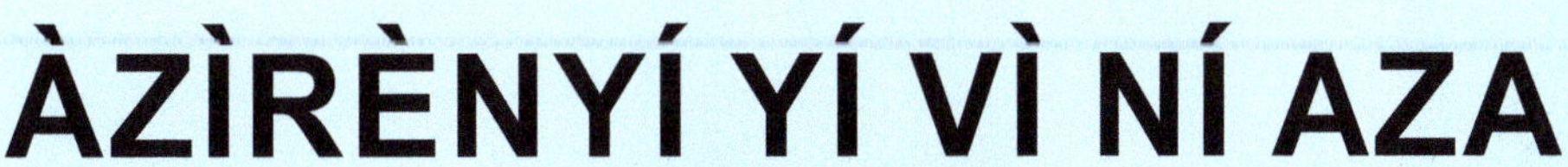

WE ARE DIFFERENT – ÀZÌRÈNYÍ YÍ VÌ NÍ AZA

Ọnọrú
Man

Ọmárî
Baldness

Ozí ọnyẹ́nẹé
Girl

Osú óchẹngwụ́/
Ọjavụ/Ọkụmị
Paraplegic

Ọ̀nyẹ́nẹé/Ọnẹẹ
Woman

Ozí ọnọrú
Boy

Ọ́chẹngwụ́
òbóóro
Full Figured/
Curvy

Jụ̀gẹjúgẹ
Slim

Ògùeyí/
Gù eyi
Blind

Bányí/Òmuhà
Ọ́bányí
Big/Giant

Wèyí
Small

Ọgọdọ
Tall

Ọnẹẹ́
Female
Onobo
Old Person
ỌnẹẹÒzọgà
Bride
Ọnọrú Ọ̀zọgà
Groom
Uzoza/Dẹẹre
Beauty/
Slender
Ọpozuéyi
Young
Ọnọrú
Male
Ohịnọyị
King
Ozí
Baby/Child
Oziohinoyi
Prince or Princess
Òsé Ohịnọyí
Queen

GREETINGS – ỤKỤ́

QUESTIONS – HÙSÈ ỊRÉYÍ/USIREYI

Sọví?
What?

Ọ̀mẹ́yà?
How?

Ènọví?
Who?

Sèvè?
Why?

Ìzòvi?
Where?

Ìhìovì?
When?

COMMANDS – Ọ́DÂ

Nâ!	Go!
Zaaje!/Jẹ̀ẹ́!	Stop/Stay/Wait
Asunâ!	Don't Go!
Navọ́!/ Kweeze!	Leave!
Nịzọọ!	Go there!
Ve!/Vịzẹ́nị!	Come!/Come here!
Sioro uyo!	Speak!
Kúrenu awụ!	Be quiet!
Yá nâ!	Let's go!
Tàngwà!	Be careful!
Yàátụ́ụ̀!	Sit down!
Jẹ̀ẹ́má sí zụ́ wụ!	Let me show you!
Batọ́!	Listen!
Vàchírê	Taller
Tẹnytẹny	Shorter
Àárịhịnị	Please
Àhẹ́	Sorry

DIRECTION – ÒZÈ

Ụvọ́ha
Left

Ụvọ́rí
Right

Ịrẹma
Behind

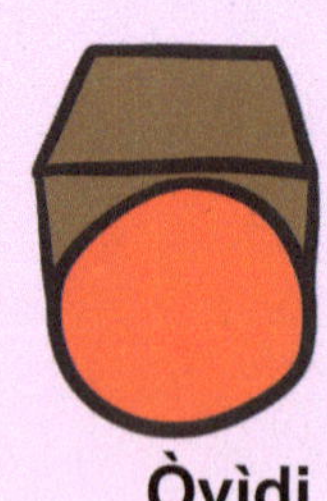

Òvìdị
In front

Ẹ̀bẹ̀ẹ̀ba
Up

Ụvẹ́tẹ
Down

Ịní ịrẹsụ́/Akeba
On top of

Ìrùvò
Under

CARDINAL POINTS –
Ọ̀GỌ̀GỌ̀ Ẹ̀Ẹ̀NÀ ẸHẸ

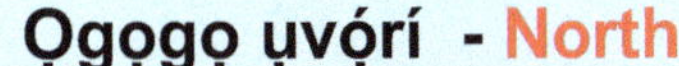

MEMBERS OF THE SKY –
ÀÀBI ỊSÁ ÀNÁ ỊNÍ Ẹ̀BÈẸ̀BA

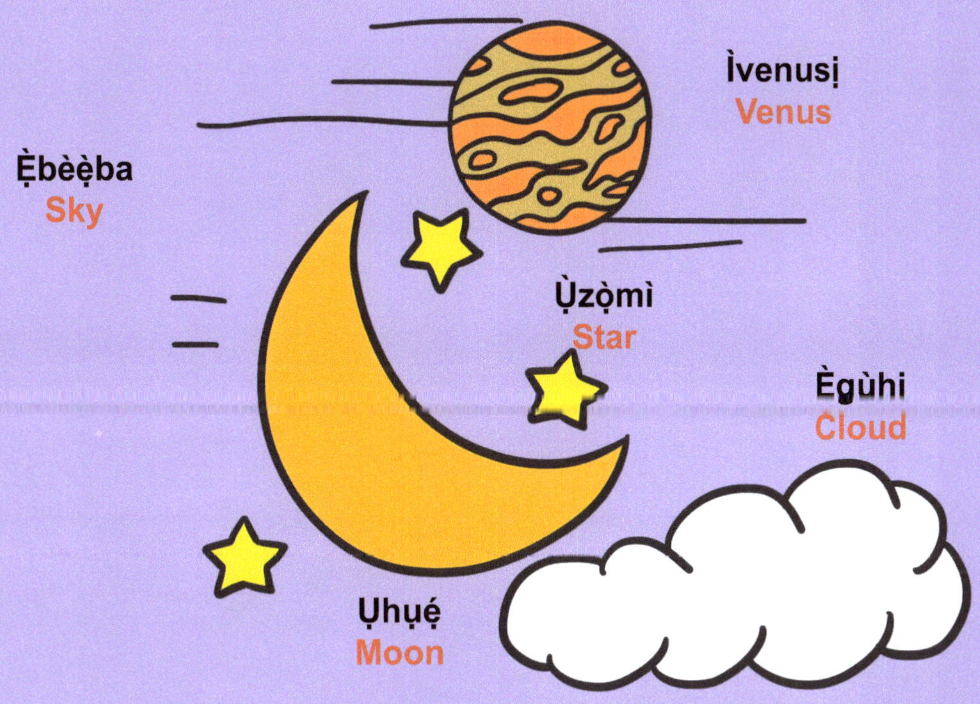

POSTURES/POSITIONS

SCHOOL – IRÉHI ÌWE

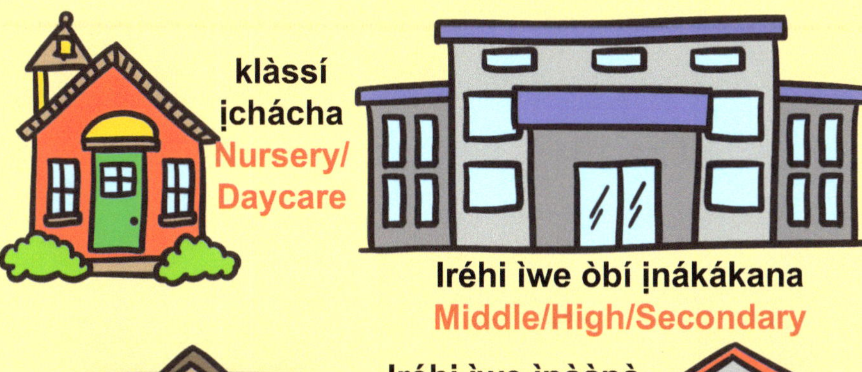

klàssí ịchácha
Nursery/
Daycare

Iréhi ìwe òbí ịnákákana
Middle/High/Secondary

Iréhi ìwe ìpààpà
Primary

Iréhi ìwe ọ̀bányí/ Ire'hi'oy-iye-obanyi (Akeba)
University

SPEAK UP
KÀRẸYỊ TÚẸHẸ

Kàrẹyị	Talk/Speak
Tú òhì	Answer
Hùsè	Question
Ée/Hịịn	Yes
Éyìyé	No
Òyísì	Love
Bàrà/ Ayamụkụ	Hate/Dislike

TIME/PERIOD – ÙMÈ ỊNÍ ẸKỤ̀HÎ

Ẹ̀nẹ́nẹ
Sunrise
(7am-11am)

Ọ̀ọ́dụ
Afternoon
(Noon-2pm)

Ọ̀ọ́dụ
Early Evening
(3pm-5pm)

Chàkúu/Etohoze
Darkness

Ẹtóhweyí
Light

Orúva
Late Evening
(6pm-8pm)

Ìrahụ́
Late Night
(9pm-11pm)

Àgévà Ìrahú
Midnight
(12-2am)

Ètuméyọ́nị
Dawn
(4am-6am)

Àchéva ịsájú	Seconds
Ịsájú	Minutes
Wàkàtị	Hours
Ẹkụhî	Days
Ọ̀sẹ́	Weeks
Ụhụẹ́	Months
Ịrayị	Years
Ajínị	Today
Ụhuọọ	Tomorrow
Ẹ̀ẹ̀rí	Yesterday

VERBS

Hee	To visit
Hèe	To find
Jẹẹ	To wait
Nyee	To wipe, clean
Nọọ	To annouce
Tọọ	to select
Zẹẹ	To Allow/ Answer
Họ	To ask
Hụrẹ ayị ịnẹ	To fear
Dà	To cut
Gọdọ	To be long
Hura	To stir
Na	To open

Jị	To cut
Mọ	To measure
Nu	To leak
Pọ	To be cheap
Re	To look
Sika	To limp
Tura	To pull
Vẹ	To come
W-weyi	To be small
Ye	To know
Za	To catch
Chaka	To break
Ngụ	To enter
Nyinyi	To laugh

PHRASES

Leave from here - Hụụ zọọ
You did not drink water - Weyi hú enyi
You have not yet drunk water - Weeyi hú enyi
If you have not drunk water - Wèeyi hú enyi
I am sick - Ẹngụ aa zị mị
I am hot - Ẹhị ee tu mi
He likes her - Óo si ịreyị ani
He is the one who did it - Ónị omẹẹ nị
I am sucking an orange - Mee hú oromi
I am going to take a bath - Maa naa hụ enyi
Where did you go today - Izụ ụ nọ ajịnị?
Look at the meat - Re uye ọnọọ!
You are eating bananas - Waa rị ọgẹdẹ
My orange - Oromi ami
How are you? - Etemeya?
I am fine - Ma dahi
Hope you are fine? - Wadahi OR Avu dahi?
How is work? - Akoro yo?
How is your father? - Inda u yo? OR Ada u yo?
How is your mother?- Inyha u yo? OR Onyha u yo?
He/she/it is fine. - O dahi
Long time no see - Anyari Ekuhi Eta
What is your name? - Ireha awu ri?
I thank God - Ma ku Ohomorihi Avo
Come and Eat - Ve Varisa
How much is this? - Oya Osoni vi?
Wait for me - Je zimi
Welcome - Nyhasẹ (from a journey),
Anyharusẹ (from a short outing)

ACTIONS

He is going hunting	Ee zu ube
He is speaking	Aa ka ịrẹyị
He is running away	Ee zue echi
He is sleeping	Aa sụ ara
He is walking	Aa zị ụsẹ
He is dancing	Aa nyị ẹzẹ
He is Boasting	Ee wo oto
I am yawning	Maa nọwa
I am belching	Maa nụhị
He is weeping	Ee nowu
He is crying	Ee sune
He is asking	Ee huse
He is Coughing	Ee suse

PRONOUNS

Ẹmị-I	Myself
Ẹwụ	You
Ọnị	He, she, it
Ẹyị	We
Ẹwụ nịnị	You
Ẹnị/Ẹnịnị	They/Their
Amị/Emi	My
Awụ/Ewu	Your
Anị	His/Her/Its

EBIRA NAMES

Uhuotu | Meaning that this world is mere a stage and we are all players or spectators to play our respective parts and roles until we die.
ASIMI | If mankind will allow me the survival of this child| Female/Male.
AJIMITUHUO | Spare me today till tomorrow, which day metaphorically continues till eternity (since tomorrow has no end)| Male.
AVIDIME | The initiator who work is subsequently perfected by those following him in life| Male.
ASIPITA | A child of history| Male/Female.
AMEWURU | The harbinger of confusion, or the man who causes chaos| Male.
ADEKU | Father of masquerade| Male.
ADABARA | Father of compound| Male.
ADAJINEGE | The tallest of them| Male.
ADAVIZE | Father of wealth| Male.

EBIRA NAMES

ADEIZA | Father of fortune/gift/kind| Male.
ADOMUHA | Father of able body man| Male.
ADOORO | The one that is a stumbling block
ADUVO | Father of hand| Male.
AJOZE | The one standing on the way| Male.
ADINOYI | The father of the multitude who serves as a protective umbrella shielding others in need of such protection| Male.
ADAVIRUKU | Name usually given to the heir of the family| Male.
ANAYIMI | That which is given or surrendered to me| Female.
AZAMARE | Test (Trial), that he who is under the test of God for survival| Male.
ANOZE | That which is delivered on the way to the farm or that which is to open the gate for others to follow| Female.
ANANWUREYI | That which is heralded by memorable events| Female.
A'AZE | Child of difficult circumstance| Female.
ENIEYAMIRE | That which the eye has seen| Male.
EZUHIO | Heralded by the many or the multitude| Male.
ENEBE | Heralded by the many or multitude| Male.
ENESI | That child which is greatly sought for, the much loved child| Male.
ITOPA | A historic child| Male.
IREYI | Heralded by some memorable events| Female.
OTUHUO | Child named after a succession of deaths of other children in a family| Female/Male.
OVAVI | Child named after a succession of previous children| Male.
ORAHACHI | One that find a place to stay| Female.
OCHIJI | Child of a termagant who is notoriously quarrelsome. Female/Male.
ONOZARE | That which is seen by the naked eye, or is God given| Female.
OSHEIZA| That which is memorable or can serve as a witness. Female/Male.
ONOTO | The one that is proud and self-centered| Male.
ONORUOIZA | Good man| Male.
ONIZE | Owner of Wealth| Female.
ONOTU | The one that is met| Male.
ONOZASI | The one people search for| Female/Male.
ONSACHI | The one that accept to be sent| Female.
ONUCHI | The one that you help to bring down the load from head| Female.
ONUME | The one in the period of time| Male.
ONUWOJI | The adviser| Male.

EBIRA NAMES

ONUYA | The sufferer| Female/Male.
ONIMISI | The one I like or the one I looked for| Male.
OMEIZA | The one that gives (gift/money)| Male.
ORICHA | That which is given or surrendered to me| Male.
OZOVEHE | Man is the symbol of life or creation| Male.
OTORI | Friend of the oracle or the shrine for worship| Male.
ONYECHE | Named after a festival, meaning the mother of festival| Female.
OMATA | Endless nature of creation| Female.
OZOMATA | As a symbolized by the name of that which is healed by hope and abundance for the future. It is the symbolism for continuity and eternal creation by God| Male.

www.ingramcontent.com/pod-product-compliance
Lightning Source LLC
LaVergne TN
LVHW070224110826
845147LV00003B/638

* 9 7 8 1 9 5 7 0 7 6 2 3 2 *